Greek Ornament

GREEK ORNAMENT

Translation and introduction by Patrick Connell

B. T. BATSFORD LTD London

First English Language Edition 1968

Introduction © B. T. Batsford Ltd 1968

Originally published in Greece under the title
Ellenika Diakosmetika Themata
© Ethnikos Organismos Ellenikes Kheirotekhnias, Athens, 1961

Made and printed in Great Britain
by Jarrold and Sons Ltd, London and Norwich
for the publishers B. T. Batsford Ltd
4 Fitzhardinge Street, London W 1

Contents

5

Acknowledgment

The publishers wish to thank the following for permission to reproduce photographs appearing between pages 11 and 28 of this book: the Ashmolean Museum, Oxford, for nos. 4–7; the Trustees of the British Museum for nos. 2, 3, 8–13, 15–24, 28 and 33; Mr Nicholas Brock for nos. 36 and 37; Mr Peter Clayton for no. 1; and the Trustees of the Victoria and Albert Museum for nos. 29–32, 34 and 35.

Page 81 is reproduced from O. Broneer, *Corinth*, vol. IV, 2, *Terracotta Lamps*, by kind permission of the American School of Classical Studies, Athens; page 82 is reproduced from G. M. A. Richter, *A Handbook of Greek Art*, by kind permission of Phaidon Press Ltd; and pages 101 and 102 are reproduced from *Byzantine Glazed Pottery*, by kind permission of the author, Professor D. Talbot Rice.

Introduction

Greece, with her origins stretching back some 5,000 years, has the longest cultural tradition in the western world. Although the Greeks have had far more than their fair share of invasions, disasters, civil strife and population movements, Greek culture has proved remarkably able, not only to endure, but through the centuries to absorb and use much valuable foreign influence, whilst still remaining truly Greek. The ability to absorb played an important role in the great flowerings of Greek civilization, whether in ancient Mycenae, Periclean Athens or the Byzantine Empire. The ability to endure kept Hellenism alive through dark times, including 400 years of Turkish rule.

A most striking continuity is, of course, the Greek language, surprisingly little changed in many ways since Homeric times. A word in a modern folksong may recall an image in the *Odyssey* or a line in a Byzantine hymn. In the same way, a pattern in contemporary peasant embroidery may remind us of a motif on a Cretan jar made over 4,000 years ago. Such is the time-span and the continuity of this book.

The many hundreds of decorative motifs here presented were originally collected into a book by the National Organization of Greek Handicraft (*Ethnikos Organismos Ellenikes Kheirotekhnias*), an official body that has done very valuable work in support of Greek crafts. Their purpose in publication was, as they said in their preface, 'to help the Greek craftsman in his work by giving him a wealth of designs to use according to his judgment. A new source of inspiration for new creations.' The aim of this English-language edition is a similar one: to provide a rich source of inspiration to all in the English-speaking world who—as professionals or amateurs—work in embroidery, textile design, woodcarving, pottery, metal craft, and so on. It is hoped that the book will also interest Hellenists, though they must perhaps be warned that the motifs, whilst often representative, have been chosen mainly for aesthetic reasons.

The Greek edition contained only the line illustrations. The present publishers, however, felt that many of their readers, although they might have a nodding acquaintance with the Elgin marbles or the characteristic ancient black-figure vases, would lack the Greeks' familiarity with some of the sources of the motifs, whether Minoan jars or Byzantine pottery or peasant embroidery. Accordingly, thirty-seven plates have been added to show typical vessels, coins, textiles, carvings, capitals, etc., of all periods. These photographs thus impart a third dimension to the book.

The early pages are mainly concerned with the predecessors of the Greek race, in the Cyclades and in Crete, during the third and second millennia B.C. The Cyclades (Section I) are the inner ring of Aegean islands to the north of Crete, and include

Syros, Paros, Naxos, Amorgos, Santorin (ancient Thera) and Milos. Our knowledge of Cycladic culture is largely based on clay pots and marble vases, particularly found in tombs. Plates 1–3 and page 36 show examples of their shapes, which are mostly simple, with the interesting exception of the *kernos*, a ritual vase (plate 2; figs. 7 and 8 on page 36). Ornament is equally simple and often naturalistic, with pleasing bird and plant motifs.

There was a thriving trade between the Cyclades and Minoan Crete (Section II), and both cultures had their roots in the Middle East. However, in ancient Crete we find one of the most brilliant and sophisticated civilizations of all time. The subtle and elegant achievements of Crete in the second millennium B.C. far surpass their Egyptian inspiration. We owe the term Minoan (and much besides) to the pioneering excavations of Sir Arthur Evans at the great palace of Knossos at the turn of the present century. He chose to think of Knossos as the home of the legendary king Minos, the owner of the Minotaur and the persecutor of Theseus and the Athenians, a ruler of fabled wealth and power. Certainly the prevalence of bulls and labyrinthine patterns in Minoan decoration—labyrinth from *labrys*, a double axe—show some basis for the legends (see plate 27, bottom; pages 40, 54 and 55).

Evans' discoveries gave the first glimpse of an amazing world of great palaces, luxury, wealth, fashionable ladies, plumbing and baths. Ornament keeps pace with the rest of the civilization. The Cretan artist was chiefly inspired by nature, by plants and flowers, by animals—birds, fish, octopuses—and by the decorative forms derived from them (see, particularly, plates 9–12). Page 58 and plates 4–8 show typical pottery shapes on which they appear, but the motifs are taken from many other sources—for instance, from jewellery, sarcophagi, frescoes, seals and baths.

In Section III we see the climactic rise of the racial Greeks. Just how and why they arrived in mainland Greece from the early second millennium B.C., ousted Minoan power and subsequently imposed their domination and language in Crete itself, is a huge and complex question. Suffice to say here that they did so. The Greeks of the Mycenaean age adopted Minoan culture and artistic traditions, though they gradually evolved an art of their own. However, their most impressive legacies are the mighty citadels and 'beehive' tombs at Mycenae (plate 14) and Tiryns—suitable homes perhaps for Agamemnon and the sackers of Troy.

The Mycenaean age (roughly 1400–1150 B.C.) was succeeded by a dark period of chaos and further Greek invasions. When after some 300 years the mists clear and the institutions of Classical Greece first begin to take shape, the 'Geometric' period of art has commenced. 'Geometric' vases are surrounded by continuous bands of circles, semi-circles, wavy lines, zigzags, nets, triangles, lozenges and meanders (plate 16). Soon the bands opened up to let in figure decoration (plates 17 and 19)—horses, deer, birds, mythical beasts, and so on—and from there it was a further step to the Classical black- and red-figure pottery with its characteristic scenes from mythology and heroic times (plates 22–24). But ornament of the geometric sort persisted in Classical and post-Classical pottery, and indeed was important in many other forms of art. The Classical period in the sixth and fifth centuries B.C. developed many new motifs—rosettes, chequers, scrolls, spirals, eggs, tongues, rays, lotus flowers, palmettes, scales and guilloche —and the Hellenistic centuries that followed continued the tradition. Throughout we see the Greek capacity for taking over what appealed in the art of other times and other races, and making new creations. Many of the motifs had been used in Egypt, Assyria and Crete, but they were now transformed into typically Greek designs of grace and lightness.

Section IV is entirely devoted to the coins of the ancient Greek world. This needs no excuse since, as Richter says in the splendid *Handbook of Greek Art*, 'the coins of Greece are in some ways her most characteristic product'. The large number of independent city-states and colonies widespread around the Mediterranean and Black Sea made for a huge variety of designs. Many cities used animals or plants as symbols of their local deities; the most famous example is, of course, the owl of Athena, patron goddess of the city of Athens (plate 27). Later on we find appearing heads or figures of deities themselves, of heroes, and so on. Coins are normally of gold, silver, bronze or electrum.

With Section V we turn from the pagan world of the ancient Greeks to the Christian Empire of Byzantium. In the intervening period much had happened. Athens declined and Macedon rose. Alexander the Great of Macedon spread an impermanent empire and an abiding Greek culture all round the eastern Mediterranean, before his death in 323 B.C. In 146 B.C. Greece was at last saved from internal strife when she became a Roman province. But though conquered by the Romans Greece soon in turn dominated the culture of her conquerors. Consequently, after Constantine in A.D. 330 moved his capital from Rome to the city of Byzantium (henceforward, Constantinople), we are not surprised to find the Eastern Roman Empire becoming Greek in language and in most other ways.

Byzantine power endured for more than 1,000 years, until the fall of Constantinople to the Ottoman Turks in 1453. It was, of course, a highly religious empire, and most Byzantine art was religious in purpose or inspiration. In Section V we find motifs taken from church architecture and church furniture, from icons, mosaics, ivories, bronzes, psalters, and much else. Plates 28–33 show examples of Byzantine ornamental work in pottery and other artefacts. We can see rich influences from the Moslem empires of the East joining with the Greco-Roman tradition to produce new and satisfying styles.

Section VI and plates 34–37 are concerned with the folk crafts of modern Greece. Here it is difficult to make any proper generalizations about the style of ornament. One can, of course, point to the continuing inspiration received from nature. There are animals, birds and plants, presented with differing degrees of naturalism and schematization, appearing on the examples of embroidery, weaving, woodcarving and other distinctive products. However, by this stage one has all the weight of the long tradition, and the thorny problem of to what extent it has been self-consciously or naturally followed. There are, too, wide regional variations, and the related foreign influences— Italianate, Slav, Turkish, and so on—that, in true Greek style, have been moulded into a living and exciting culture—the oldest in the western world.

9

Select Bibliography

Arias, P., Hirmer, M. and Shefton, B.B. *A History of Greek Vase Painting*, London, 1961

Beazley, J.D. *The Development of Attic Black Figure*, London, 1951

Buschor, E. *Plastik des Griechen*, Munich, 1958

Cook, R.M. *Greek Painted Pottery*, London, 1960

Demus, O. *Byzantine Mosaic Decoration*, London, 1947

Diehl, C. and Hame, A. *Manuel d'Art Byzantin*, Paris, 1926

Ghali-Kahil, L. *La Céramique Grecque*, Paris, 1960

Glazier, R. *A Manual of Historical Ornament*, 6th ed., London, 1948

Head, B.V. *A Guide to the Principal Coins of the Greeks*, London, 1959

Jacobsthal, P. *Greek Pins*, Oxford, 1956

Johnstone, P. *Greek Island Embroideries*, London, 1961

Jones, O. *The Grammar of Ornament*, London, 1856

Lane, A. *Greek Pottery*, London, 1958

Meyer, F.S. and Stannus, H. *A Handbook of Ornament*, London, 1894

Millet, G. *Monuments Byzantins de Mistra*, Paris, 1910

Petrie, W.M.F. *Decorative Patterns of the Ancient World*, London, 1930

Richter, G.M.A. *A Handbook of Greek Art*, London, 1959
    Archaic Greek Art, Oxford, 1949

Seltman, C. *A Book of Greek Coins*, London, 1952
    Greek Coins, London, 1955
    Approach to Greek Art, London/New York, 1948

Wace, A.J.B. *Mediterranean and Near Eastern Embroideries from the Collection of Mrs F.H. Cook*, London, 1935

1, Marble vases from the Cyclades, *c.* 2500 B.C.

2, 'Kernoi' (ritual vases) from Milos, *c.* 2000 B.C.

3, Cycladic jug, probably from Milos, 1850–1700 B.C.

4, Jug from Crete, 2400–2100 B.C.

5, Spouted jar from Knossos,
1900–1700 B.C.

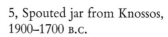

14

6, 7, Cups from Knossos
1900–1700 B.C.

8, Large storage jar from Knossos, 1450–1400 B.C.

9–12, Goblets, 1400–1300 B.C. Goats facing tree from Crete,
the others from Ialysos, Rhodes

13, Gold bowl, probably from Crete, 1550–1500 B.C.

14, Stonework from the façade of a royal tomb at Mycenae (the so-called 'Treasury of Atreus'), 1350–1250 B.C.

15, Jar in Protogeometric style, *c.* 1050 B.C. Probably from Athens

16, *above:* Jug in Geometric style, 900–800 B.C. Probably from Athens

17, *above right:* Cycladic jug in 'orientalizing' style, 700–650 B.C.

18, *right:* Clay Gorgon head, architectural decoration from Taras (Taranto), south Italy, c. 450 B.C.

19, Water-jug from Laconia (Sparta), 580–550 B.C.

20, *below left:* Lid of a clay trinket box from Athens, 600–500 B.C.

21, *below:* Fish-plate from south Italy, 330–300 B.C.

22, Inside of Athenian goblet,
red-figured, 490–480 B.C.

23, Athenian amphora,
black-figured, 540–530 B.C.

24, Jar from south Italy, red-figured, *c.* 375 B.C.

25, 'Ionic' capital from temple of Artemis (Diana of the Ephesians) at Ephesus, *c*. 550 B.C.

26, Part of North Doorway of the Erechtheum n Athens, 420–395 B.C.

27, Silver coins bearing emblems of Greek cities. *Top, left to right:* Metapontum, south Italy (barley), *c*. 530 B.C.; Akragas (Agrigento), Sicily (crab), *c*. 520 B.C.; Metapontum, 330–300 B.C.; Athens (owl standing on amphora), third century B.C.; *bottom:* Knossos (labyrinth), second century B.C.

28, *above left:* Gold cross set with sapphire, sixth century A.D.

29, *left:* Jasper pendant, *c.* A.D. 900

30, *above:* Carved elephant tusk, eleventh or twelfth century A.D.

31, Byzantine glazed jar, tenth or eleventh century

32, Byzantine glazed bowl, thirteenth or fourteenth century

33, Page from a Byzantine illuminated manuscript, twelfth century

34, Embroidered skirt
border, silks on linen, Crete,
seventeenth or eighteenth
century

35, Embroidered borders
from the Greek islands,
seventeenth or eighteenth
century

36, Cushion cover, tapestry
weave in coloured wools on
plain sacking material, 1946

37, Bread stamp, 1964

I

CYCLADIC

1, Jug from Phylakopi, Milos, 2000–1700 B.C. 2–4, Bone whistle and clay boxes from Syros, 2400–2000 B.C. 5, Jar from Santorin, 1700–1400 B.C. 6, 7, Cups from Phylakopi, 2400–2000 B.C.

32

1, Jug with incised decoration from Syros.   2–4, Jugs and jar from Phylakopi, Milos.   5, Sauce-boat from Naxos. All 2400–2000 B.C.   6, Vase from Phylakopi, 2000–1700 B.C.

1, 2, Jug and amphora from Phylakopi, Milos, 2400–2000 B.C.   3, 4, Clay boxes from Syros, same period.   5, 6, Vases from Phylakopi, 2000–1700 B.C.   7–9, Jugs from Amorgos, Lerna (Argolid) and Phylakopi, same period.

1–3, 5, Jugs.   4, Large jar. All from Phylakopi, Milos, 1700-1400 B.C.

1–3, 8, Jugs. 4, Cup. 6, Amphora. 5, 7, Unknown shapes. All from Phylakopi, Milos, 2000–1700
B.C. (3, Phylakopi style, found at Lerna, Argolid.)

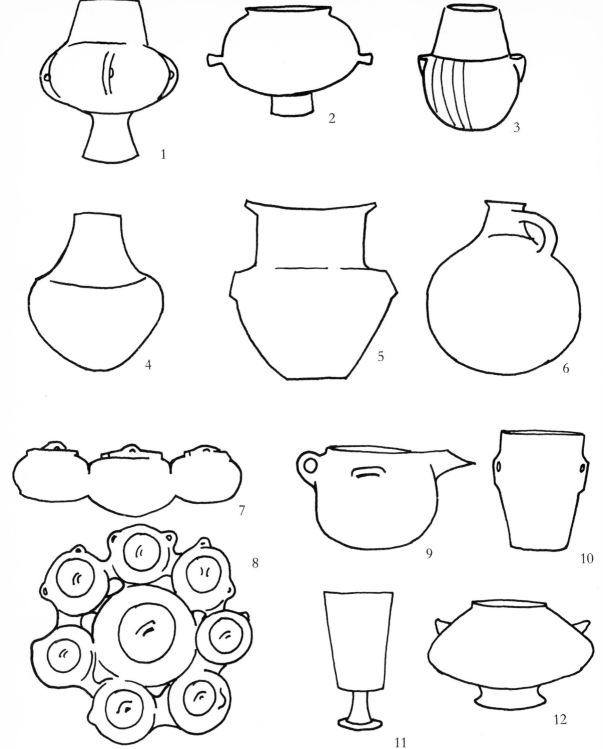

Representative shapes of Cycladic vessels

1, 2, Vases of Parian marble from Antiparos and Amorgos. 3, 4, Clay jars from Paros and Antiparos. 5, Clay jar from Amorgos. 6, Clay jug from Naxos. 7, 8, Clay 'kernos' (ritual vase) from Syros. 9, Clay jar with spout from Santorin. 10, Marble jar from Paros. 11, Alabaster cup from Santorin. 12, Clay jar from Amorgos. All 2600–2000 B.C., except 9, 2000–1700 B.C.

II

MINOAN

1, Vessel from Mallia. 2, 8, 9, Ivory seals from Platanos and Marathokephalo. 3, Steatite seal from Hagios Onouphrios. 4, Jug from a tomb at Mochlos. 5, 6, 10, 11, Stone vases from Platanos and Pseira. 7, Frying-pan-shaped clay utensil from the Cyclades, 2500–2200 B.C. All Cretan, 2400–2100 B.C., except 7.

1, 2, Jugs from Hagia Triada and Palaikastro.   4, 5, Cup and libation-jug from Phaistos.   6, 7, Jars from Pseira. All *c.* 1500 B.C.   3, 8, Vases from Phaistos, 1900–1700 B.C.

1, 5, 6, 8, 9, Cups. 2, Jug. 3, Amphora. 4, Jar. 7, Steatite vase. All from Phaistos (except 6, from Knossos), 1900–1700 B.C.

1–5, 10, 11, Cups. 6, Vessel. 7, Fruitstand. 8, 9, Jars. All of the period 1900–1700 B.C. All from Phaistos, except 8 (from Kamares Cave).

1, 4, Inside of fruitstands. 2, Strainer. 3, Cup. 5, Amphora. 6, Jar. All from Phaistos, 1900–1700 B.C.

1, Steatite vase from Phaistos. 2, Rock-crystal seal from Mochlos. 3, Steatite seal from Knossos. 4, 5, Jar and cup from Phaistos. 6, 7, Large jars from Phaistos. All 1900–1700 B.C.

1, 4, Three-handled jars from Phaistos, 1900–1700 B.C.   2, Jug from Phaistos, same period.   3, Jug from Phaistos, *c.* 1500 B.C.   5, Basket-shaped jar from Pseira, 1500 B.C.   6, Bath from Pachyammos, 1350 B.C.

46

1, Jar from Mochlos, 1580–1450 B.C. 2, Goblet from Psychro, same period. 3, 5, Amphoras from Knossos, *c.* 1400 B.C. 4, Vessel from Palaikastro, *c.* 1500 B.C. 6, 7, Trinket-box and bath from Pachyammos, thirteenth century B.C.

1, Apron of a faience goddess from Knossos, 1600–1580 B.C. 2, 4, Sarcophagus from Anogeia, fourteenth century B.C. 3, Fresco from the palace of Knossos, 1580-1450 B.C. 5, Decoration on a bronze double axe from Arkalochori, 1700–1580 B.C. 6, Representation of a helmet on a vessel from near Knossos, 1425–1400 B.C. 7, Stand of a porphyry lamp from Knossos, 1550 B.C. 8, Cup from Phaistos, 1900–1700 B.C.

48

1, Ivory ornament from the palace of Knossos.   2, Fresco from the palace of Tiryns, 1400 B.C.
3, Vessel from Pseira.   4, Vessel from Nirou Chani.   5, Ivory ornament from Palaikastro.   6,
Haematite seal from Mochlos.   7, Sardonyx seal from Praisos.   8, Libation-pourer from Knossos,
1450–1400 B.C.   9, Pitcher from Slavokambos.   10, Cup from Knossos. All of the period 1580–
1450 B.C. except 2 and 8.

1, Jug from Mycenae, 1580–1500 B.C.   2, 3, Shoe-shaped vessel from Voula, Attica, fourteenth century B.C.   4, Amphora from Kakovatos, Triphylia, 1500–1425 B.C.   5, Bowl from Amnisos, Crete, thirteenth century B.C.

50

1, Jug from Palaikastro, 1500 B.C.   2, 3, 6, Libation-jugs from Pseira, same date.   4, 5, Amphora from Knossos, 1425 B.C.   7, Decoration on a sarcophagus from Palaikastro, 1400–1350 B.C.

Vessels from Rhodes

1, Cup, unknown date. 2, 4–6, 11, Mycenaean vases, 1350–1300 B.C. 3, Amphora, *c.* 550 B.C.
7, 8, Seventh century B.C. 9, Sixth century B.C. 10, Eighth century B.C.

52

1, Fresco from Tiryns, 1400 B.C.   2, Three-handled amphora from Knossos, *c.* 1430 B.C.   3, Sarcophagus from Anogeia, thirteenth century B.C.   4, Cretan jug (the 'Marseilles Ewer'), *c.* 1500 B.C.
5, Jar from Prosymna (Argolid), 1500 B.C.   6, Jug from Phylakopi, Milos, 1700–1580 B.C.

1, Vessel from Phaistos, *c.* 1300 B.C.   2, Trinket-box from Pachyammos.   3, 4, Sarcophagus from Milatos.   5, Sarcophagus from Episkopi Hierapetras.   6, 7, Sarcophagus from Pachyammos. 8, Jug from near Knossos, *c.* 1400 B.C. All of the thirteenth century B.C. except 1 and 8.

54

1, Jug from Knossos, 1400 B.C.   2, Example of linear script from Knossos, same date.   3, Bead in the form of two sea-snails, common in Crete and mainland Greece in gold and in blue glass, four-teenth century B.C.   4, 5, Clay bath from Gournia, 1350–1300 B.C.   6–8, Clay phials from Phaistos, c. 1300 B.C.

55

1, 2, Vessels from Cyprus, 1300–1200 B.C.   3, 4, Amphoras from Boeotia, 700–650 B.C.   5, 6, Vases from Phaistos, 1580–1450 B.C.   7, Goblet from Palaikastro, same period.

1, 2, 4, Mycenaean jugs, fourteenth century B.C. 3, Same, twelfth century B.C. 5, Mycenaean goblet, thirteenth century B.C. 6, 7, Mycenaean bowl, *c.* 1200 B.C. 8, Gold brooch, ninth century B.C. 9, Bowl from Boeotia, early seventh century B.C. 10, 11, Attic amphora, same date.

1, Blue glass bead, Mycenaean, *c.* 1300 B.C.   2–4, Silver brooches, fourth century B.C.   5, 6, 8, 9, Gold ear-rings, fourth and third centuries B.C.   7, 12, 13, 15, Gold ornaments from Mycenae, 1600–1500 B.C.   10, Gold pendant, late third century B.C.   11, Gold ring, fifth century B.C.   14, Gold ornament from Crete, 1400–1200 B.C.

58

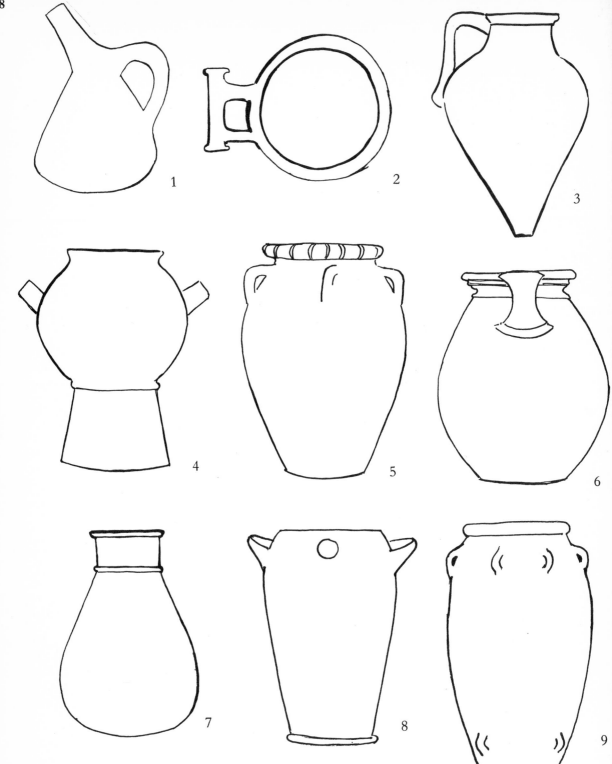

Representative examples of Minoan ware

1, Spouted jug from central Crete, 2700–2500 B.C. 2, Frying-pan-shaped utensil, 2400–2100 B.C.
3, Pitcher from Phaistos, 1500 B.C. 4, Footed basin from Zakro, Crete, 1550 B.C. 5, Large jar from
Phaistos, 1500 B.C. 6, Amphora from Knossos, 1700 B.C. 7, Clay phial from Phaistos, 1300 B.C.
8, Jar from Knossos, 1600–1580 B.C. 9, Large storage jar from Phaistos, 1900–1700 B.C.

III

MYCENAEAN
GEOMETRIC
CLASSICAL
HELLENISTIC

Rhodes

1–3, 6, 8, Plates and cups, 650–600 B.C. 4, 'Geometric' vessel, eighth century B.C. 5, 7, Jug and cup, Mycenaean period, *c.* 1350 B.C. 9, 10, Large jar, Mycenaean period, *c.* 1450 B.C.

1, 2, 4–10, Motifs from 'Geometric' vases, mostly Attic, eighth century B.C. 3, Corinthian jug in 'orientalizing' style, 725–700 B.C. (8 and 9 are shields.)

1, Athenian funeral urn, eighth century B.C. 2, Athenian bowl in Proto-Attic style, early seventh century B.C. 3, Athenian amphora, *c.* 540 B.C. 4, 5, 'Geometric' cup from Attica, late eighth century B.C. 6, 'Geometric' amphora from Boeotia, 700–650 B.C.

1, Corinthian wine-jug, 700 B.C.   2, 4, Seventh-century vase motifs, various sites.   3, Proto-Attic water-jug, 675–650 B.C.   5, 6, 8, Vases from Rhodes, 650–600 B.C.   7, Fruit-bowl from Chios, seventh century B.C.

1–4, Amphora from Santorin, early seventh century B.C.   5, 6, Wine-jug from Attica, c. 750 B.C.
7, 8, Corinthian wine-jug and scent-bottle, 700 B.C.   9, Cycladic jug, c. 650 B.C.

1, Trinket-box from Cyprus, seventh century B.C.   2–4, Proto-Attic amphora, 670–650 B.C.   5, Amphora from Euboea, 700–650 B.C.   6, Amphora from Milos, c. 660 B.C.   7, 10, Motifs widespread in the seventh and sixth centuries B.C.   8–9, Goblet from Laconia, c. 600 B.C.

1–7, Rhodian vases, seventh century B.C.   8–9, Rhodian vases of the Mycenaean period, *c.* 1400 B.C.

68

1–3, 6, 7, 9, Proto-Attic vases.   5, Bowl from Argos.   4, 8, Amphora from Milos. All of the
seventh century B.C.

1–8, Athenian amphora, *c.* 550 B.C.: Herakles and the Stymphalian birds (British Museum).

1, 2, 4, 5, Border patterns on Attic vases, 540–500 B.C.   3, Motif on couch legs in vase paintings, sixth and fifth centuries B.C.   6, Cup from Sardis, *c.* 700 B.C.   7, 9, 'Caeretan' jug of 525 B.C., perhaps made in Etruria.   8, Border pattern on Attic vases, fifth century B.C.

1, Water-jug from Attica, 470–460 B.C.   2, Bottle from Thebes, 640 B.C.   3, 4, Vessel from Laconia, 540 B.C.   5, A common motif on Athenian wine-cups, 530–500 B.C.   6, 'Chalcidian' water-jug, perhaps made in Etruria, 540–530 B.C.   7, Fruit-dish from Rhodes, 625–600 B.C.   8, Athenian amphora, *c.* 520 B.C.   9, Attic amphora, 540 B.C.

1, Ionian goblet, 550 B.C.   2, Textile pattern, and 3–7, Running border patterns on Athenian vases, sixth century B.C.

1, Common motif round base of vases, seventh to fifth centuries B.C. 2, Vine pattern on Attic amphora, 540 B.C. 3, 4, 6, 7, 9, 11, Textile patterns from vase paintings, same date. 5, Motif on furniture in Attic vase paintings, sixth and fifth centuries B.C. 8, Corinthian and Laconian vases, 575–550 B.C. 10, Motif from sixth- and fifth-century vases.

1–3, Patterns on garments and on a helmet, Attic amphora, 525 B.C.   4, Attic amphora, 520 B.C.
5, Heraldic device on a shield, Attic cup, *c.* 510 B.C.   6, Textile pattern on Attic bowl, 510–500 B.C.
7, Palmette and lotus border on sixth-century Attic vases.   8, Lyre in Attic vase paintings.   9,
Helmet decoration from an Attic cup, *c.* 455 B.C.   10, Palmette border pattern on Attic bowl,
450 B.C.

1, 2, Water-jug from Laconia.   3, 5, Chalcidian water-jugs, perhaps made in Etruria.   4, 'Caeretan' water-jug, perhaps made in Etruria.   6, Furniture motif from Attic vase.   7, Cup from Laconia. All 565–510 B.C.

1, Laconian water-jug, 540 B.C. 2, 3, Laconian cup, 600–575 B.C. 4, Vine pattern on Attic vases, sixth century B.C. 5, 'Caeretan' water-jug, perhaps made in Etruria, 540–530 B.C. 6, Amphora from Attica, 520 B.C. 7, Attic amphora, c. 530 B.C.

1, 2, 13, Corinthian vessels, sixth century B.C. 3, Furniture motif in an Attic vase painting, *c*. 480 B.C. 4, Border pattern on Attic vases, late sixth century B.C. 5, Amphora from Attica, 520 B.C. 6–9, Plate from Rhodes, end of seventh century B.C. 10, Goblet from Laconia, *c*. 550 B.C. 11, 12, Amphoras from Attica, 520 B.C. 1, 2, 5, 7, 8, 11 and 13 are heraldic devices on shields in vase paintings.

1–4, Border patterns from Attic vases, fifth century B.C.   5, Same, sixth century B.C.   6, Scale pattern used in vase painting as a textile pattern and also to represent scales on armour and sea-monsters—Attic, sixth and fifth centuries B.C.   7, Textile pattern on an Attic cup, *c.* 460 B.C.   8, Attic amphora, 500 B.C. (represents leopard skin).   9, Attic and south Italian vases, 440–400 B.C.

1–3, Textile patterns in Attic vase paintings, sixth and fifth centuries B.C. 4, 5, Border patterns on Attic and south Italian vases, fifth century B.C. 6, Sculptured relief on north door of the Erechtheum at Athens, c. 420–395 B.C. 7, 8, Coffered work on the Propylaea of the Acropolis, Athens, 437–432 B.C. 9, Sculptured relief in the Tholos at Epidaurus, c. 360–320 B.C.

80

1–3, Patterns on armour and 4, Dagger on Attic bowls, 460–450 B.C. 5, Textile pattern on an Attic wine-jar, *c.* 430 B.C. 6, Attic amphora, *c.* 400 B.C. 7, Textile pattern on an Attic cup, *c.* 400 B.C. 8–11, Etruscan bowl, *c.* 340 B.C.

1–28, Decorations on Corinthian clay lamps of Hellenistic type, 44 B.C. to A.D. 14.

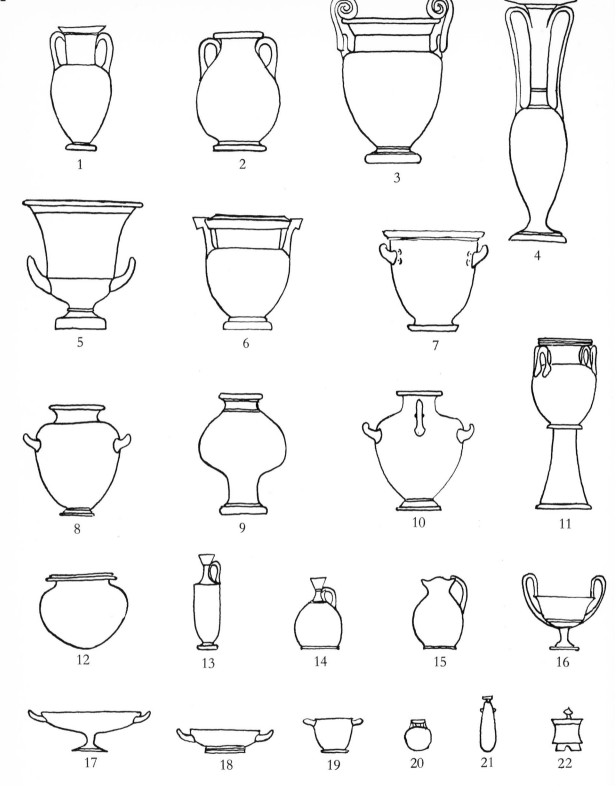

Typical shapes of vessels of the sixth and fifth centuries B.C.

1, Amphora.   2, 8, 12, Other wine-jars.   3, 5–7, Bowls for mixing wine and water.   4, Tall ewer.
9, Cooling jar.   10, Water-jug.   11, Bowl used in marriage ritual.   13, 14, Oil-flasks.   15, Wine-jug.   16–19, Cups and goblets.   20, 21, Small scent-jars.   22, Box for jewellery or trinkets.

IV

COINAGE

1, Knossos, sixth century B.C. 2, Tarantum (wheel), sixth century B.C. 3, Kroton, Sicily (tripod), *c.* 520 B.C. 4, Lycia, *c.* 470 B.C. 5, Salamis, Cyprus, 480–460 B.C. 6, Cyrene (silphium plant), 400 B.C. 7, Apollonia Pontica (anchor), fifth century B.C. 8, Maroneia, *c.* 430 B.C. 9, 10, Mende, 450–425 B.C. 11, Delphi, 480 B.C. 12, Aegina, 480–460 B.C. 13, Aegina, 350–320 B.C. 14, Syracuse, *c.* 350 B.C. 15, Syracuse, *c.* 300 B.C. 16, Hierapytna, Crete, *c.* 360 B.C. 17, Macedonia, third century B.C. 18, 19, Knossos, (labyrinth), second century B.C. All silver except 14 (bronze) and 15 (electrum).

1, Kameiros (fig leaf), 600 B.C.   2, Elis, Olympia, fifth century B.C.   3, Haliartos, sixth century B.C.
4, Salamis, Cyprus, *c.* 500 B.C.   5, 7, Himera, Sicily, sixth century B.C.   6, Ionian Revolt, 499 B.C.
8, Sicyon, sixth and fifth centuries B.C.   9, 10, Zankle, Sicily, *c.* 500 B.C. All silver except 6 (electrum).

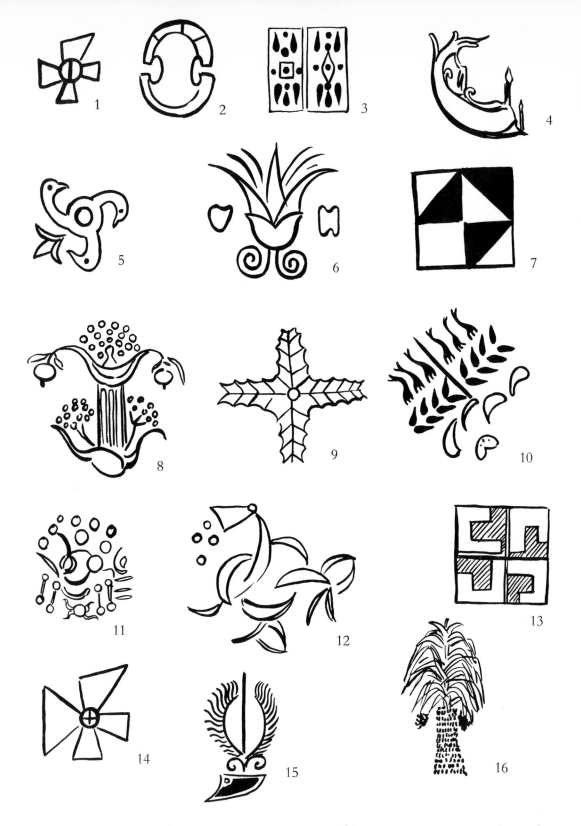

1, 2 (shield), 14, Boeotia, sixth century B.C.   3, Corcyra (Corfu) same century.   4, Scione (stern of ship), 470 B.C.   5, Lycia, 460 B.C.   6, Idalium, Cyprus (lotus), 460 B.C.   7, Milos, 450 B.C.   8, Cyrene (silphium plant), 500 B.C.   9, Rhodes, 350 B.C.   10–11, South-west England.   12, Yorkshire, c. 100 B.C., degenerate versions of Macedonian coins.   13, Corinth, 600 B.C.   15, Catania Sicily (thunderbolt).   16, Carthage, 406 B.C. All silver except 9–12 (gold).

1, Argos, *c.* 530 B.C. 2, Corinth, *c.* 640 B.C. 3, Himera, Sicily, *c.* 520 B.C. 4. Lycia, *c.* 460 B.C.
5, Delphi (dolphins and ram's heads), 478 B.C. 6, Elis, Olympia, *c.* 480 B.C. 7, 8, Metapontum,
c. 410 B.C. 9, Elis, Olympia (thunderbolt of Zeus), *c.* 420 B.C. 10, Rhodes, 408 B.C. 11, Naxos,
Sicily, 490 B.C. 12, Sybaris, *c.* 530 B.C. 13, Kroton (Herakles and tripod), 430 B.C. All silver.

1, Itanos, Crete (sea-serpent), *c.* 400 B.C.   2, 3, Athens, fifth century B.C.   4, Adranum, Sicily, *c.* 345 B.C.   5, Sidon, *c.* 367 B.C.   6, Olynthos, 360 B.C.   7, Ptolemy XIII of Egypt, 60 B.C.   8, Athens, 176 B.C.   9, Methymna, 425–400 B.C.   10, Dyracchium (Durazzo) *c.* 280 B.C. All silver except 4 (bronze).

1, 4, Elis, Olympia, *c*. 450 B.C.   2, Corinth, *c*. 450 B.C.   3, 5–7, Akragas (Agrigentum), Sicily, *c*. 450 B.C.   8, same, *c*. 420 B.C.   9, Troezen (trident of Poseidon), *c*. 450 B.C. All silver.

V

BYZANTINE AND LATER
RELIGIOUS ART

1, Illuminated border from psalter of the ninth century A.D.
A.D. 1118.   4, Mosaic in the Chora church, Istanbul, *c.* 1310.
centuries.   7, Part of a metal cross.

2, 3, Mosaics in Santa Sophia, Istanbul,
5, 6, Ear-rings of the sixth and seventh

1, Decorative marble slab, twelfth century.   2, Relief of the twelfth century.   3, Icon of A.D. 1130.
4, Piece of woven silk, A.D. 800.   5, Piece of woven silk, eighth century (Victoria and Albert
Museum, London).   6, Psalter of the ninth century.   7, Mosaic in the Chora church, Istanbul,
c. 1310.

Mystra, Peloponnese

1, Top of the central apse in the Pantanassa church. 2, South-west dome of the Pantanassa. 3, Hagia Kyriaki chapel of the Perivleptos church. 4, Cornice of the west apse of the Perivleptos. 5, Arch of the east door of the Perivleptos. 6, Decoration in the Perivleptos. 7–9, Fresco in the Perivleptos. 10, Painted decoration in the Metropolis church. 11, Decoration. 12, Nave of the Pantanassa. 13, Table in the vestry of the Metropolis. 14, Church of the Vrontocheion monastery. All fourteenth century.

Mystra

1, Decoration representing a candlestick. 2, From a south window of the Evangelistria church. 3, Window-column in the main apse of the Metropolis church. 4, Carved floor-slab in the Metropolis. 5, Carved monogram of Manuel Cantacuzene in the Pantanassa church. 6, Buttress of the dome of the Perivleptos church. 7, Buttress of the nave in the Hagia Sophia church. 8, Altar window in the Pantanassa. 9, Buttress of the dome of the Perivleptos. 10, Window decoration in the Pantanassa. 11, Ironwork from a tomb in the Vrontocheion monastery. 12, Outside cornice of the main apse of the Perivleptos. All fourteenth and fifteenth centuries.

1, Embroidery on ecclesiastical dress, 1696.   2, From 'epitaphion' (Good Friday shroud), Ankara, 1682.   3, Same from the Soumela monastery, Asia Minor, 1738.   4, 5, Eucharistic veil of the end of the eighteenth century.

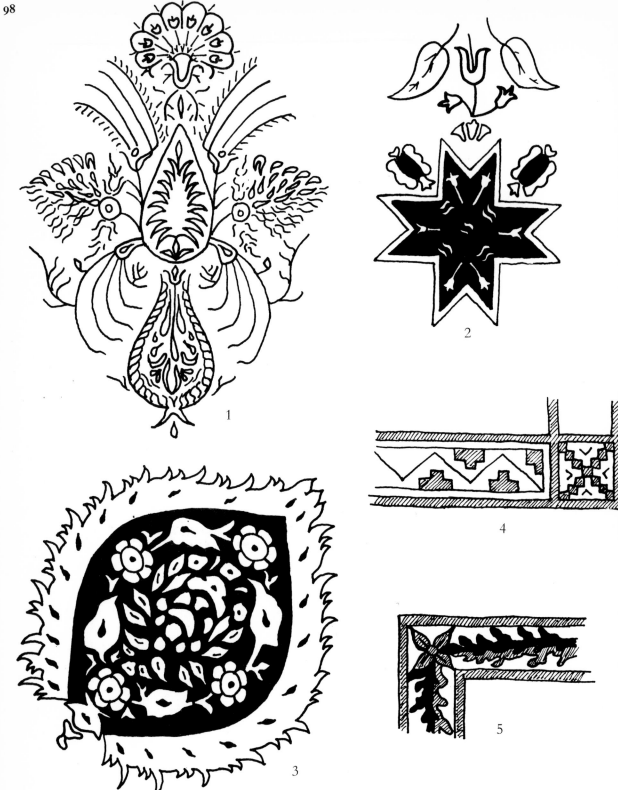

1, 2, Eucharistic veils of the end of the eighteenth century.   3, Same, 1664.   4, 5, From illuminated manuscripts, tenth century.

1–6, Reliefs in the Byzantine Museum, Athens.

1-5, Marble reliefs in the Byzantine Museum, Athens.

Monograms (mainly fourteenth-century Imperial from ceramic ware)

1, 2, 15, Berlin Museum.   3, 6–9, 11, 13, 14, 16–19, 22–25, Istanbul Museum.   4, 12, St. George's Museum (the Rotunda), Thessalonica. 5, 10, Talbot Rice Collection, London. 20, 21, Odessa Museum.

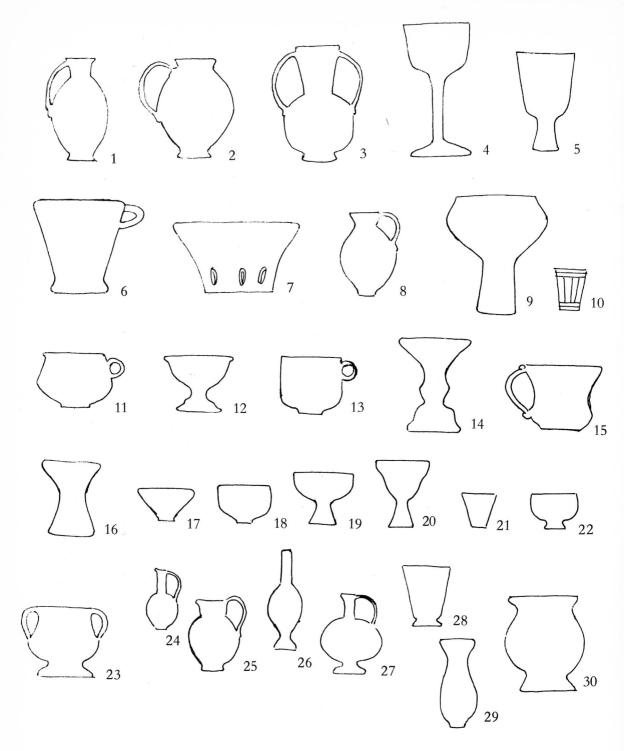

Typical shapes of Byzantine vessels

1, 2, 8, 24, 25, Pitchers.   3–5, 9–11, 13, 15, 17–22, 28, Cups and glasses.   6, Strainer.   7, Brazier.
12, Salt-cellar.   14, Glass shaped like a water-clock.   16, Egg-cup.   23, Vessel with handles.
26, 27, Flasks.   29, Tall vase.   30, Pitcher without handles.

1–16, From the Talbot Rice Collection, London.   17–30, From frescoes on Mount Athos.

VI

FOLK ART

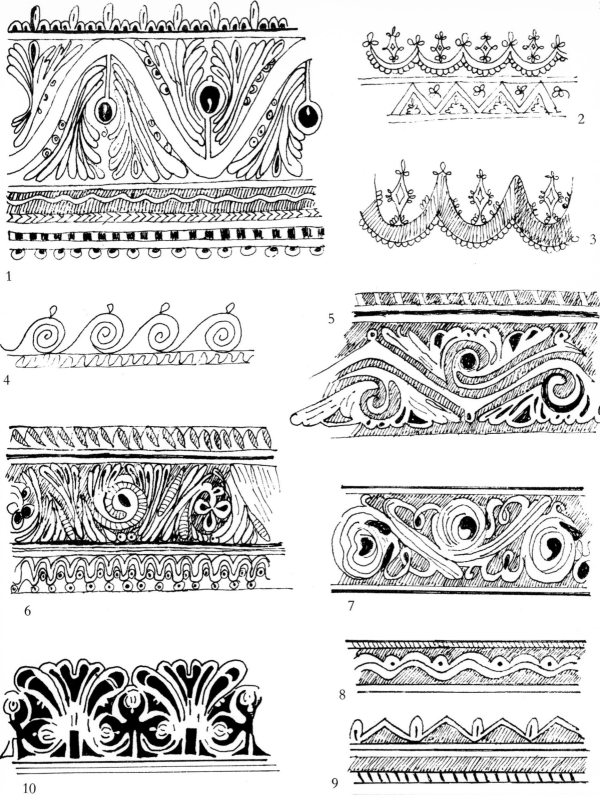

1, Embroidered sleeve. 2–4, 8, 10, Embroidery motifs. 5–7, Embroidery on man's costume.
9, Cord decoration. Macedonia, all but 4 being from the village of Roumlouki.

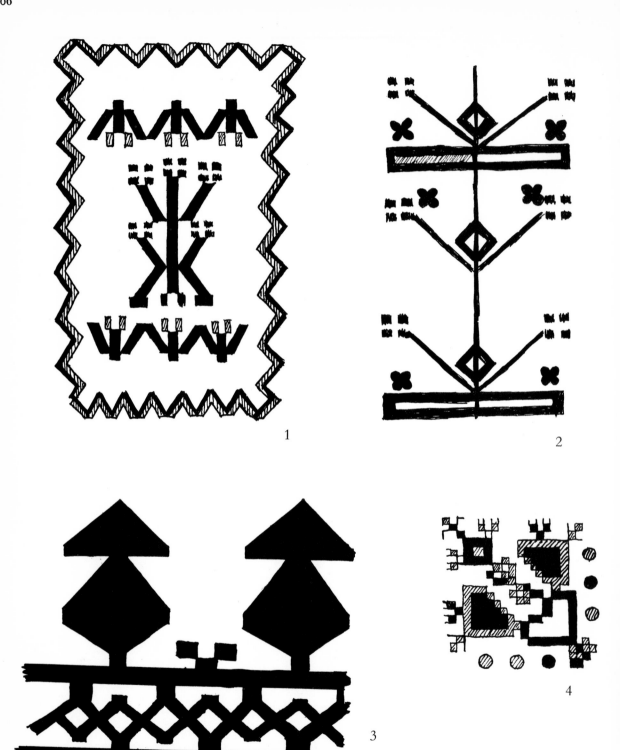

1, Cushion in shaggy wool, from Roumlouki.   2, 3, Embroidery on traditional shirt from Roumlouki.   4, Border motif, man's costume from Trikeri, Thessaly.

Embroidery motifs

1, From a woman's costume. 2, From a slipper. 3, From a shirt. 5–8, Border motifs. All from the village of Trikeri, Thessaly.

1–8, Embroidery motifs from Trikeri, Thessaly.

1–8, Embroidery motifs from Trikeri, Thessaly.

Embroidery motifs

1, 3–5, Sarakatsan (primitive nomad people of northern Greece). 2, Macedonian. 6, From the island of Thasos. 7–9, On towels from central Crete.

1, 2, Towels from Crete.   3, Folk-weave from Crete.   4–7, Sarakatsan aprons.

1, Ship on crêpe. 2, 3, Lace. 4–6, Embroidered sheet (Museum of Decorative Arts, Athens).
All from the island of Skyros.

1, Eagle.   2, Double eagle.   3, Wooden seal.   4, Eagle on a headscarf.   5–8, Birds on costumes.
9, Carved wooden box. All from Skyros.

Embroidery from Skyros

1, Tulip on a costume.   2, Tapestry chain.   3, 6, Sheets.   4, 5, 'Spark' and 'branch' motifs.

Embroidery from Skyros

1, Costume.   2, 'Little Monastery' motif.   3–6, Sheets.

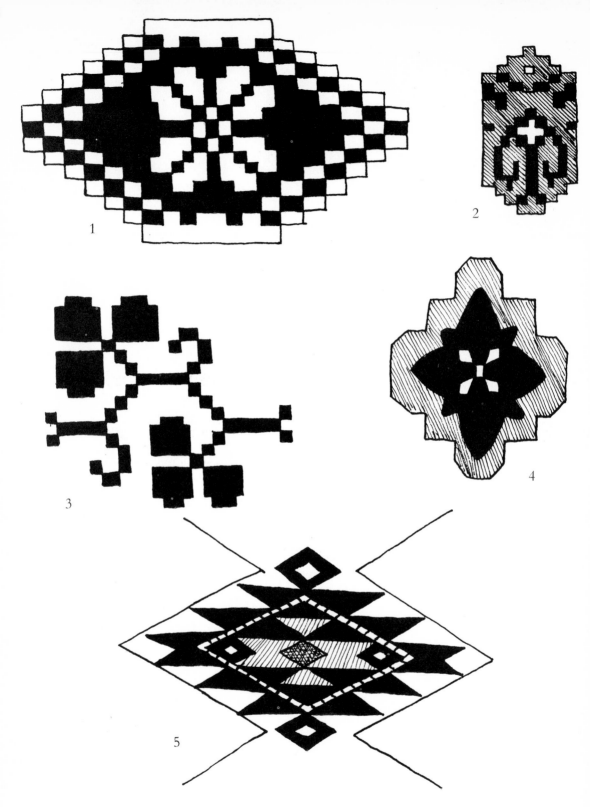

1, Woven rug from Epirus. 2, Woven apron from Souphli, Thrace. 3, 4, Woven rugs from Argos. 5, Peasant's bag (woven) from Attica.

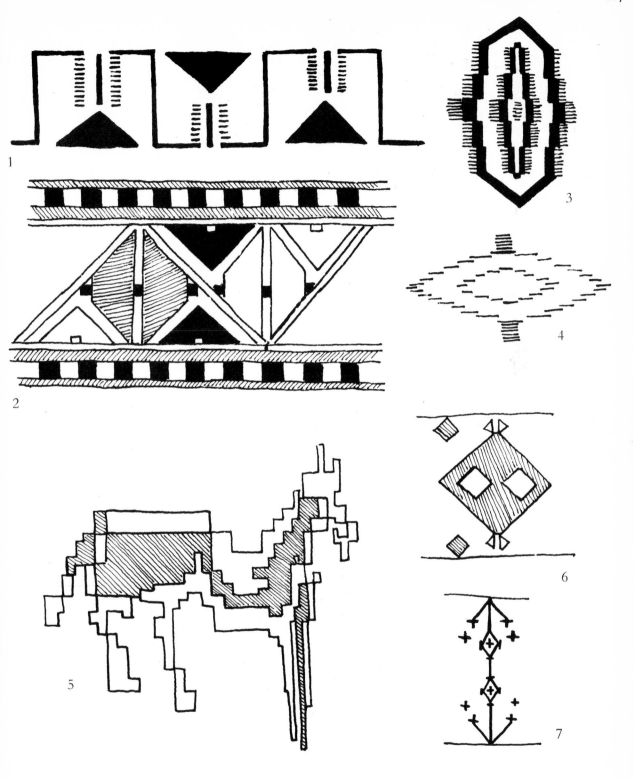

1, Woven blanket from Arta, Epirus. 2, 6, 7, Cushion covers from Rethymnon, Crete. 3, 4, Folk-weaves from Ypati, near Lamia, central Greece. 5, Woven rug from Epirus.

118

1, 2, Woven towels from Khania, Crete.   3–5, Woven rug from Lesbos.

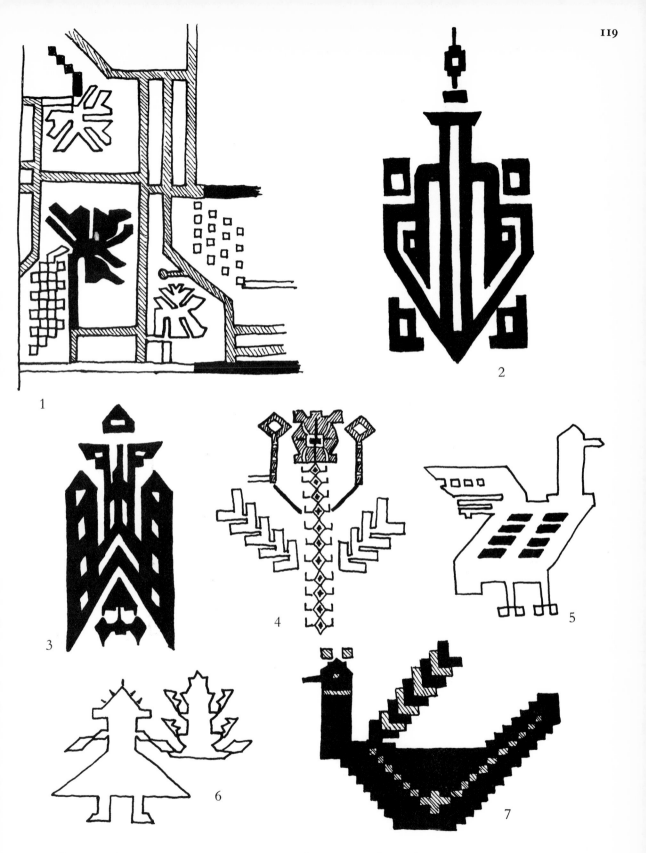

1, Folk-weave from Rethymnon, Crete. 2, 3, Small woven rug from Khania, Crete. 4, 5, Woven towels from Anogeia, central Crete. 6, 7, Peasants' bags (woven) from Rethymnon, Crete.

1, 2, Woven rug from Lesbos. 3, Embroidery from Nauplia. 4, Towel from Rethymnon, Crete.
5, Towel from Herakleion, Crete.

1, 2, Folk-weave from Herakleion, Crete. 3, 4, Woven blankets from Crete. 5, 6, Embroidery from Arakhova, near Delphi. All of the sixteenth, seventeenth and early eighteenth centuries, and all in the Museum of Decorative Arts, Athens.

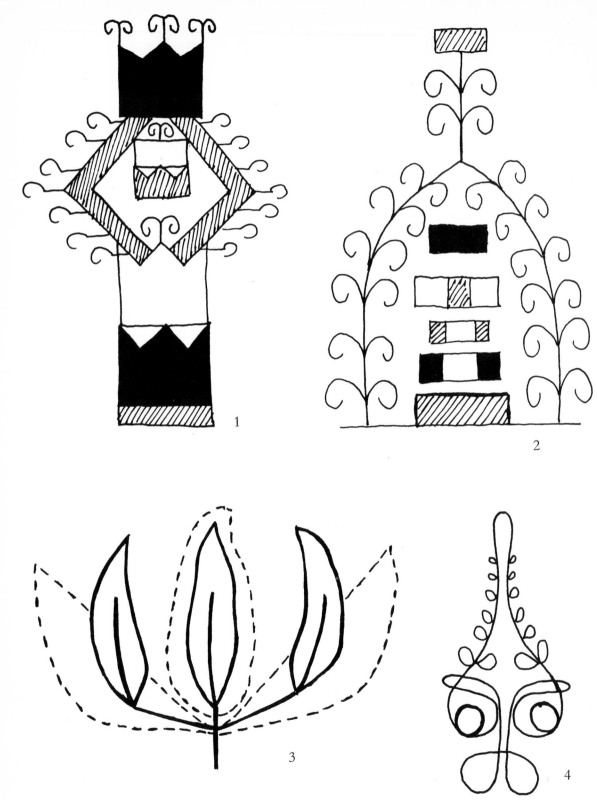

1–4, Antique embroidery on Epirote costumes.

Carved wood

1–5, From Mesolonghi.   6, 7, Distaff from Corfu.

124

Carved wood

1–5, Tobacco-boxes from Mesolonghi.   6, 8, Small chair from Skyros.   7, Small table from Skyros.

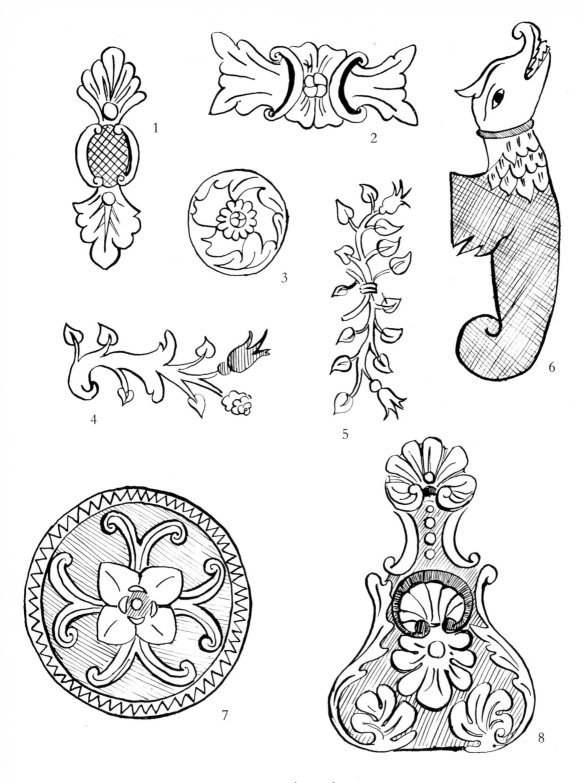

Carved wood

1–5, Door from Portaria, Mount Pelion, Thessaly.   6, Armrest of a bench from Portaria.   7, Door from the island of Siphnos.   8, Lamp-stand from Siphnos. All from the photograph archive of the Museum of Decorative Arts, Athens.

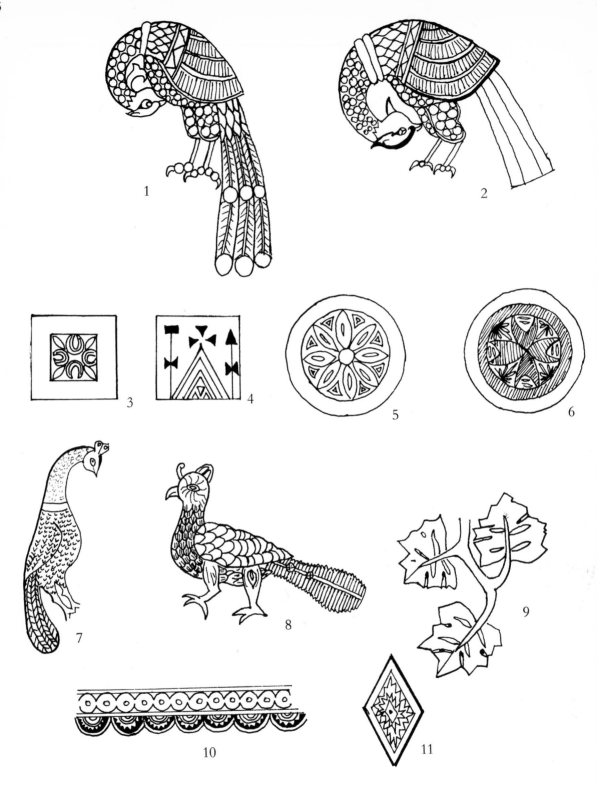

Carved wood

1–3, Khania, Crete. 4, Seal from Mount Athos. 5, 6, Salonica. 7–9, Chests from Metsovo, Epirus. 10, 11, Distaff from Corfu.

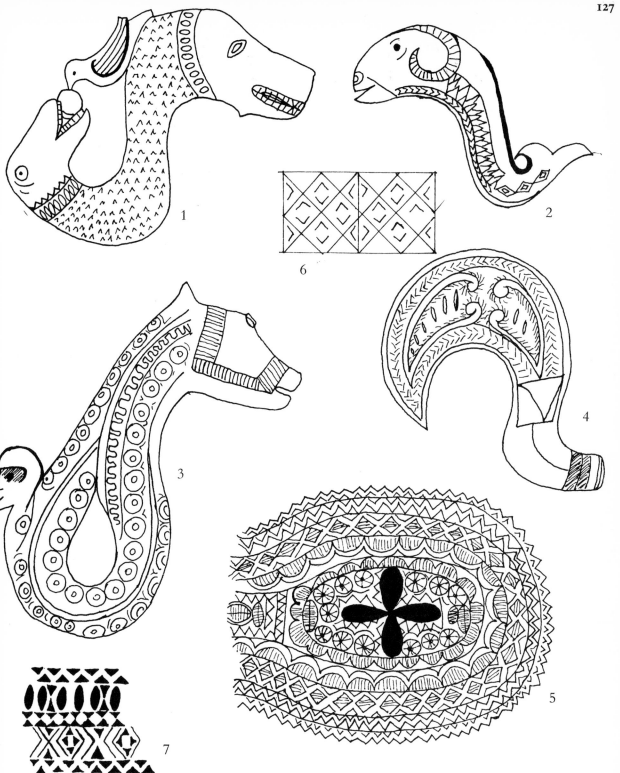

Carved wood

1, 2, 4, Shepherds' crooks from Mount Pelion, Thessaly. 3, Shepherd's crook from Levadia, central Greece. 5, Distaff from Larissa, Thessaly. 6, Bowl from Dodona, Epirus. 7, Distaff from Skyros.